Usher
Hip-Hop and Beyond

capstone
classroom

BTR Zone (Bridge to Reading) is published by Capstone Classroom,
1710 Roe Crest Drive, North Mankato, Minnesota 56003
www.capstoneclassroom.com

ISBN: 978-1-62521-074-6

Editorial Credits

Kristen Mohn, editor; Ashlee Suker, designer; Eric Gohl, media researcher

Photo Credits

Alamy: AF Archive, 18; AP Photo: Mark Duncan, 39; Dreamstime:
Imagecollect, 4; Getty Images: Usher's New Look Foundation/Michael
Loccisano, 40, The Washington Post/Robert A. Reeder, 7, WireImage/KMazur,
9, 10; iStockphotos: EdStock, 42; Newscom: AdMedia/Jackson Lee, 26, Splash
News/Janet Mayer, 41, UPI/David Silpa, 36, UPI Photo Service/Bill Greenblatt,
17, UPI Photo Service/Ezio Petersen, 12, ZUMA Press/Pool, 28, ZUMA Press/
UPPA, cover, 15; Shutterstock: Debby Wong, 20, 33, DFree, 30, Featureflash,
22, 34, s_bukley, 25

Design Elements: Shutterstock

About the Cover

Usher performs in London for the 2001 MOBO (Music of Black Origin) Award

Direct Quotations

pp. 16-17: quoted in *USA Weekend*, August 7-9, 1998
pp. 20-21: quoted in *Ebony Magazine* interview, June 2004
pp. 28-29: quoted from usherworld.com

Printed in the United States of America in North Mankato, Minnesota.
032013   007223CGF13

TABLE OF
CONTENTS

Usher and Jonetta in 2005

CHAPTER 1

Born to Sing

On October 14, 1978, Jonetta Patton named her newborn son Usher Terry Raymond IV. Throughout his career, her son gave himself nicknames, such as Big Time and Mr. Entertainment. The world knows him today by just one name: Usher.

Usher has always enjoyed singing. By the time he was 6 years old, he was already quite good. While growing up in Chattanooga, Tennessee, he sang in his mom's gospel choir. He spent many hours practicing and performing. This helped his voice get stronger. Usher's grandma was the first to think he could be really great someday. She was right. Usher became so great he grew up to sing for U.S. presidents.

Gospel Music

Gospel music is a type of powerful Christian music sung by one person or by a whole choir. It can sound a little like the blues or jazz. Gospel music has become so popular that some singers put out their own gospel records.

New Beginning

At age 11 Usher joined the musical group Happy Clowns. These boys sang and did acrobatic (tumbling) stunts. They were not very popular, so they changed their act. The group switched to performing **Motown** (upbeat blues) hits and dance moves. The boys also changed their name to Nu Beginning. As part of this band, Usher recorded 10 songs to make an album (record). It was called *Nu Beginning Featuring Usher Raymond IV*. At first the album was only sold by **mail order**. Later a record **label** (company) called Hip-O Records signed Nu Beginning to a **contract**. The company helped to sell the album to more fans.

When he was 12 Usher's family moved from Chattanooga to Atlanta, Georgia. Usher was unhappy about having to leave his band, but the move helped Usher's career. Atlanta is a hot town for music, so it was a great place for a young singer. With lots of hard work Usher started to build a reputation. He also met important musicians and other people in the music **industry** (business).

Motown · upbeat bluesy music from Detroit, Michigan; great for dancing

mail order · shopping by sending an order form and money in the mail

Usher at age 19

label · a company that hires musicians to make records

contract · an agreement to do something

industry · a set of businesses that make a living the same way

Moving Up

When Usher was 13 he appeared on the TV talent show *Star Search*. During the show he held one note for 12.1 seconds! This had never been done before. A **producer** who found talent for LaFace Records heard Usher sing. He was so impressed he signed Usher to a contract. Usher recorded the song "Call Me a Mack" for LaFace. It became part of the *Poetic Justice* movie **soundtrack** in 1993.

In 1994 singer and music producer Sean "Puffy" Combs helped Usher make his own album. He called it *Usher* and it sold well. Combs knew Usher was going to be successful and wanted the world to meet him. He took Usher to wild adult parties. Usher was under 16 and backed off from this lifestyle. He appreciated having Combs as a **mentor** (teacher). But Usher knew he did not want to have such a wild image.

producer · a person who finds and helps talent for a record label

soundtrack · the recorded music of a movie or play

mentor · a wise and faithful adviser or teacher

Usher and Sean "Puffy" Combs in 2002

Usher performing in 1997

Growing Pains

Usher had a big problem in his teen years. Like all boys going through puberty, his voice changed. Some said his career was over. But Usher knew better and so did Puffy Combs. They worked with Usher's new voice and created a sound that would grow with him.

As Usher's new voice grew, so did his star power. He made more **contacts** (connections) in the music industry and did more music for movies and TV. He recorded "Dreamin'" for the *Rhythm of the Games* album. This album was sold to raise money for the 1996 Olympic Games in Atlanta. That year Usher also recorded the song "I Swear I'm in Love." This song was used on the soundtrack for the movie *Kazaam*. Throughout his rise to fame, Usher stayed true to his goals. He created an image for himself as a cool and likeable singer.

contact ·business connection

Usher clowning around after being nominated for the "Best Male R&B (rhythm and blues) Performance"

single · one song from an album; often played on the radio to get a new album noticed

gold · a record/album that sells 500,000 copies

CHAPTER 2

My Way

With the help of producer Jermaine Dupri, Usher made the album *My Way*. He lived at Dupri's house for six months to do the work. There he learned a smooth rhythm and blues style, sometimes just called R&B. He wrote five of the songs on the album himself, including "Babyface." The **single** "You Make Me Wanna" became the number one song in the United Kingdom. It reached number two in the United States and stayed there for weeks. Usher's next big hit, "Nice and Slow," became his first number one single in the United States.

My Way was a huge success. It sold many copies, first going **gold** and then **platinum**. Usher won some major awards for this album, which also received several **Grammy** award nominations (votes) in 1998. After starring in the album's video, Usher became a major **heartthrob**. Teens around the world had a crush on him.

---

platinum · an album that sells 1 million copies
Grammy · an award for achievement in the music industry
heartthrob · a person who teens crush on; often a star

Big Names, Big Hits

Usher went on **tour** with some big stars. He opened concerts for singer Janet Jackson. He sang with Puffy Combs and **rapper** and songwriter Mary J. Blige. Performer Lil' Kim also joined him on stage. Usher's sound worked great with all these artists. From this amazing tour, Usher got the motivation to make his next album, *Live*. In 1999 he was one of *Teen People's* "21 Hottest Stars Under 21."

On his next album, *All About U*, Usher recorded mostly love songs. Yet the album got no love in the United States. Usher and his team fine-tuned it and changed the title to *8701*. It was re-released and became much more successful. The song "U Remind Me" hit number one in the United States, France, Belgium, the United Kingdom, New Zealand, and Australia. Three other songs from the album were also big hits around the world.

tour · a trip made by musicians to perform in various places

rapper · a muscian who performs rap music

Usher on tour in London in 2001

Bold Moves

Usher loved performing for his fans. He loved singing, dancing, and putting on a good show. He also loved doing what many singers could not do—writing songs. But there were other things Usher also wanted to do, and one of them was to be an actor. Usher got his first chance in 1996. He was cast as Jeremy Davis in the popular TV show *Moesha*. He did such a great job that the *Moesha* staff included his character in more episodes.

In 1999 Usher joined the cast of a TV **soap opera** called *The Bold and the Beautiful*. He played a flashy pop star named Raymond. Playing this character was not a big stretch for Usher, since he was a pop star in real life. But acting in this daytime show was a big deal. Millions of fans in countries all over the world watched it every day. Appearing in this show made Usher even more popular. It helped him build his reputation as an actor and a singer.

soap opera · a television series showing characters in overly dramatic ways

"I'm looking to be a triple threat: acting, singing, and dancing." —Usher

Usher talking to a fan in 1998

A New Role

Usher's first movie role was in a **sci-fi** horror film called *The Faculty*. He played a high school student who suspects that some of his teachers might be dangerous **aliens**. Next Usher showed his comedy skills in the film *She's All That*. He played a funny student who reports news and **gossip**. Usher's first starring role came in the movie *Light it Up*. In this **drama** he played a high school student who gets in trouble. Playing all of these different roles showed Usher's acting talent.

Usher and Rosario Dawson in *Light It Up*

Usher's acting skills were noticed. He was chosen to play singing legend Marvin Gaye in the TV show *American Dreams*. Gaye lived a complex and troubled life. Usher used his strong singing and acting skills to bring the role to life.

Acting became so important to Usher that he told *People* magazine it was his new love. He said acting was so satisfying he was thinking about leaving singing. But he kept his music fans happy and continued to sing.

sci-fi · short for science fiction; a story about life in the future or on other planets

alien · a creature not from Earth

gossip · talk or rumors about other people, often untrue or unkind

drama · a story full of action or strong feelings

"My feeling has always been that *Confessions* would be a landmark album for me." —Usher

Usher and Alicia Keys at a charity event in 2010

crunk · a style of hip-hop music featuring call and response

CHAPTER 3

Tracks of Success

Fans wanted more music from Usher, and he responded with the album *Confessions*. This album had four number one singles, including one with musician Alicia Keys. *Confessions* seemed to be about Usher's love life. Fans really connected with the song's emotional ups and downs. In 2004 Usher won two American Music Awards for this album. Then it went platinum—nine times!

The song "Yeah!" was one of the biggest hits from *Confessions*. Yet it wasn't part of the original plan for the album. Usher had thought that all the songs for *Confessions* had been chosen. But some people from the record company said it needed another big song. Usher asked rapper-producer Lil Jon for help. Lil Jon said, "Yeah!"

Lil Jon created a cool mix of **crunk**, which is a southern rap style, and R&B for the song. Five writers worked on the words, and Usher recorded the song with Lil Jon and Ludacris. This team effort paid off big time. "Yeah!" was number one for 12 weeks. It was Billboard's Hot 100 Best Song of 2004.

Usher at the nominations announcements for the
44th Annual Grammy Awards

Together

Usher continued to team up with other musical artists. In 2007 he joined R. Kelly to create the Grammy-winning song "Same Girl." To build interest in the song, they produced a hit music video. Usher also wrote and performed songs with Mary J. Blige. They worked together on the **ballad** (love song) "Shake Down" for her 2007 album, *Growing Pains*.

The **soulful** (heartfelt) title song on Usher's fifth album, *Here I Stand*, was for his wife, Tameka Foster. Other songs on the album showed that Usher's love life was not perfect. This album did not sell as well as the others. Some **critics** (reviewers) didn't like Usher's new sound.

Omarion

Usher and singer Omarion remixed Omarion's song "Ice Box." Omarion said it was very special for him to work with a big star in the music industry like Usher.

ballad · a romantic song; often slow
soulful · filled with spirit or feelings of love
critic · a person who tells the good and bad of something (often art)

Believer in Bieber

Usher respected Puffy Combs as a mentor. Usher hoped he would be a mentor someday too. That day came when Justin Bieber arrived in Atlanta. A talent manager named Scooter Braun had discovered Bieber. Braun thought it would be a good idea if Bieber met Usher. The two met in Atlanta, where Bieber sang for Usher. Later Usher watched Bieber's videos. Usher knew that Bieber was talented enough to make it big. He signed Bieber to a record contract and guided and **nurtured** Bieber throughout the various stages of stardom.

Usher liked watching Bieber go through the teen heartthrob stage. It reminded him of his early years as a teen star. He especially enjoyed the look of shock on Bieber's face when his fans screamed for him.

nurture • to care for and help grow

Usher and Justin Bieber at the Nickelodeon 2009 Kids' Choice Awards

Usher at the 2006 Broadway opening of *Chicago*

Screen + Stage = Superstar

In 2005 Usher went back to star on the big screen. The movie *In the Mix* had action, crime, and comedy. Usher handled this mix well. He also did the soundtrack, which was the first album from his record label, US Records.

Then Broadway called. Usher was asked to play the character Billy Flynn in the **musical** *Chicago*. He found that preparing to be in a live performance was very difficult but also very rewarding. Critics didn't hate his performance, but they didn't love it either.

Getting some harsh reviews from critics did not stop Usher. He still wanted to act. In 2012 he won a role in *Hands of Stone*. This movie was about boxing star Roberto Duran. In order to play Duran's big boxing **rival**, Sugar Ray Leonard, Usher had to get into buff boxing shape.

musical · a show with singing and dancing
rival · someone you compete against

Michael Jackson

Usher admired Michael Jackson's music, style, and moves. Usher respected how Jackson put his own cool twists on pop music. When Jackson died, Usher sang "Gone Too Soon" at the funeral. He had to choke back tears to finish.

"When I am writing a ballad, I am more introspective. I have to be in an environment of lots of party energy when creating a club track." —Usher

CHAPTER 4

Revolutionary Sound

Usher made his next album *Raymond v. Raymond* during a period of personal hard times. He and his wife, Tameka Foster, were splitting up. They battled over who had legal control of their boys, Usher V and Naviyd. Usher described the album as a tug-of-war between man and woman.

Critics were a bit harsh in their reviews of the album, but fans loved it. The songs "Hey Daddy" and "More" were pretty big hits. But the song "OMG" was beyond big. It ruled the charts for weeks all over the world. MTV named "OMG" the best song of 2010. Usher did 92 shows for the OMG Tour. It was his first big tour since 2004. Fans called it a major **comeback**.

comeback · a return to a former position

But Usher wasn't done with this theme. He produced eight new songs and called this longer album *Versus*. He told fans it was the last word on his life with his ex-wife. The single "DJ Got Us Fallin' in Love" with Pitbull was a huge hit. It was an upbeat start to Usher's new life.

Usher in Los Angeles with his sons, Usher V and Naviyd

Usher's Chart-Topping Mix of Styles

Usher's music has been called mainstream (popular with many) and crossover (switching styles). He has won awards and topped charts using and mixing many musical styles.

Gospel	Christian church music known for very strong voices
R&B	urban, rocking, jazz-based music with a firm beat
Hip-Hop	mix of rapping, DJ-scratching, sampling (reusing other pieces of music), and beatboxing
Pop	mix of the most popular parts of rock, urban, dance, Latin, and country music
Soul	mix of gospel music and R&B
Crunk	southern hip-hop with drum machines, heavy bass notes, loud voices, and shout outs
Electronic	electric instruments playing a heavy beat and tech (computer) sounds, used in dance clubs

Newer Than New

Usher was jazzed for a new sound. He wanted to grab the new and shake up the old. He began working on a new **genre** (type) of music. He called it "revolutionary pop" because it combined several music styles to create a new sound. The result was his seventh album, *Looking for Myself*. Usher included all kinds of musical **jams** (unplanned pieces) in this album. He said he hoped everyone who listened to it would hear something they liked.

The songs on this album go deep for Usher. "Sins of My Father" is about growing up without a dad. The video for the song "Numb" provides a glimpse into some of Usher's other personal pain. This included the pain he felt when his stepson Kile Glover died in 2012. Usher also shared his pain from the divorce battles to keep his sons. Usher used his art to help deal with these struggles.

genre · a class or category

jam · unplanned music played with another person or persons

Usher performing on the *Today Show* in 2012

Usher in London in 2012

Fresh Fans

Usher did not take his fans for granted. Yet it annoyed him when they texted, tweeted, and recorded at his shows. Usher's team decided to use the communication devices to their advantage. The next tour, Looking 4 Myself, made technology a part of the show. It was set up so fans could make **avatars** on their phones. When Usher sang the song "Scream," the avatars danced with him. Fans also got to tweet at Usher and he talked back.

Usher kept his music just as fresh as his tour dates. Justin Bieber spent some time in the studio with Usher. He noticed that Usher continued to come up with new sounds on each album. Bieber commented on how Usher could continue to sing R&B songs and still be very successful. What makes Usher exceptional is his ability to keep changing things up.

avatar · a computer icon made to stand for a person

Usher and will.i.am of Black Eyed
Peas performing during halftime of

the Super Bowl in 2011

CHAPTER 5

Usher's Far Reach

Usher has become a mainstream star. He stays busy by sharing his talents everywhere he can. He served as a mentor on season nine of *American Idol*, giving advice to new vocalists. Usher surprised fans in 2011 by showing up at the Super Bowl. He sang "OMG" and football fans became Usher fans. He continues to be a guest on many talk shows. In 2013 he became a coach for the TV show *The Voice*. He told MTV News that he was really excited about it. He likes the idea that the show emphasizes what matters most for vocal performers: the voice.

His hard work has earned him lots of recognition. His song "Climax" was named the number one song of 2012. He was nominated to receive the **NAACP** Image Award in 2013. Usher continues to be nominated for Grammys and receive praise for his work.

NAACP · National Association for the Advancement of Colored People

Beyond the Music

Outside of his music and acting careers, Usher runs several businesses. One of his interests is in making delicious food. He has opened restaurants in several cities across the United States. Usher's House in Moorhead, Minnesota, is a very popular place to eat.

Usher is also a part-owner of a basketball team, the Cleveland Cavaliers. He enjoys being a part of the NBA (National Basketball Association) family and working with the team. Off the court, he and the team give back to the community of Cleveland.

Usher has also designed several **fragrances**. The Usher line comes in scents for men and women. Usher stays busy working on a mix of many things.

fragrance · perfume or cologne

Usher at a 2005 news conference announcing the new owners of the Cleveland Cavaliers

Usher working with kids at his New Look Foundation World Leadership Conference

Priceless

Usher enjoys working for fun and money, but he also knows the importance of helping others. In 1999 he started the New Look Foundation. New Look helps young people see beyond their current circumstances. Participants receive career guidance (advice) and are encouraged to become involved in serving others. This along with their education and talent help them become successful leaders.

Usher started this foundation because he wanted to make a difference in children's lives. New Look has also helped victims of Hurricane Katrina. The foundation renewed a city block in New Orleans. Usher also joined many big stars for a concert to raise money for the storm victims.

In October 2011 Usher sang at the William J. Clinton **Decade** of Difference Concert. It was set up by former president Bill Clinton to honor people who have served the public. Months later when Usher opened a new arm of the New Look Foundation in Washington, D.C., he and Clinton met again. There they participated in a panel talk (discussion) about youth leaders and public service.

Usher and Bill Clinton at the Clinton Global Initiative in 2009

decade · 10 years

Giving Back

Usher appreciates his success and does what he can to give back to society. In recent years he has become even more **civic**-minded. He helps teens prepare for the future by encouraging them to vote. In 2008 he wanted more young people to take part in the national election. He led youth rallies and organized voter registration (sign-up) drives.

He also recorded the song "Hush." This song encouraged 18- and 19-year-olds to vote. He created a YouTube video that helped to make the song popular.

"Strivers achieve what dreamers believe."
—Usher

After the election Usher joined with singers Shakira and Stevie Wonder to sing "We Are One." They sang at President Barack Obama's first **inauguration**. Usher was honored to sing at this historic event. Through hard work and determination, Usher has lived up to his **motto**, "Strivers achieve what dreamers believe."

civic · relating to citizenship

inauguration · the ceremony of putting a person in office

motto · words or saying that tell an important message

Read More

Bolte, Mari. *Justin Bieber*. Star Biographies. North Mankato, Minn.: Capstone Press, 2013.

Llanas, Sheila Griffin. *Hip-Hop Stars*. Hip-Hop World. Mankato, Minn.: Capstone Press, 2010.

Shea, Therese. *Usher*. Right On! New York: Gareth Stevens, 2011.

Internet Sites

FactHound offers a safe, fun way to find Internet sites related to this book. All of the sites on FactHound have been researched by our staff.

Here's all you do:
Visit *www.facthound.com*
Type in this code: 9781625210746

 Check out projects, games and lots more at
www.capstonekids.com

Glossary
of Text Features

Text Feature	How to Use It
Caption: A word or group of words shown with a picture or illustration	Read a caption to understand information that may not be in the text.
Diagram: A drawing that shows or explains something	Examine a diagram to understand steps in a process, how something is made, or the parts of something.
Glossary: List of key terms with their meanings	Look up key terms in the glossary to find their meanings and to get a better understanding of the topic of the text.
Index: Alphabetical list of key terms, names, and topics in a text with their page numbers	Use the index to find pages that contain information you are looking for.
Map: A drawing that represents a place, such as a country or city	Use a map to understand relative locations and determine where events took place.
Photograph or Illustration: Visuals that are created by cameras or drawn	Examine photographs and illustrations to better understand ideas in the text that might be unclear.
Subhead: Word or group of words that divides the text into sections and tells the main idea of a section	Use subheads to locate information in the text and understand how a text is organized.
Table: Represents data in a small space	Examine a table to understand data or to compare information in the text.
Table of Contents: List of the major parts of the book and their page numbers	Use a table of contents to locate general information in the text and see how the topics are organized.
Text Box: A box in the text that provides extra information about a topic	Read a text box to understand interesting or important information.
Text Style: Bold, color, or italic words in the text	Pay attention to bold, italic, and color words to figure out which words in the text are important.
Timeline: Shows events in the order in which they occurred	Use a timeline to understand the order in which events occurred or how one event led to another.

Glossary

alien (AY-lee-uhn) · a creature not from Earth

avatar (AV-uh-tahr) · a computer icon made to stand for a person

ballad (BAL-uhd) · a romantic song; often slow

civic (SIV-ik) · relating to citizenship

comeback (KUHM-bak) · a return to a former position

contact (KAHN-takt) · business connection

contract (KAHN-trakt) · an agreement to do something

critic (KRIT-ik) · a person who tells the good and bad of something (often art)

crunk (kruhngk) · a style of hip-hop music featuring call and response

decade (DEK-aid) · 10 years

drama (DRAH-muh) · a story full of action or strong feelings

fragrance (FRAY-grents) · perfume or cologne

genre (ZHAHN-ruh) · a class or category

gold (GOLD) · a record/album that sells 500,000 copies

gossip (GOSS-ip) · talk or rumors about other people, often untrue and unkind

Grammy (GRAM-ee) · an award for achievement in the music industry

heartthrob (HART-throb) · a person who teens crush on; often a star

inauguration (in-aw-gyuh-RAY-shun) · the ceremony of putting a person in office

industry (IN-duh-stree) · a set of businesses that make a living the same way

jam (JAM) · unplanned music played with another person or persons

label (LAY-buhl) · a company that hires musicians to make records

mail order (MAIL or-der) · shopping by sending an order form and money in the mail

mentor (MEN-tor) · a wise and faithful adviser or teacher

Motown (MOH-town) · upbeat bluesy music from Detroit, Michigan; great for dancing

motto (MOTT-oh) · words or saying that tell an important message

musical (noun) (MYOO-zuh-kuhl) · a show with singing and dancing

NAACP · National Association for the Advancement of Colored People

nurture (NUR-cher) · to care for and help grow

platinum (PLAT-n-uhm) · an album that sells 1 million copies

producer (pruh-DOO-ser) · a person who finds and helps talent for a record label

rapper (RAPP-er) · a muscian who performs rap, a type of music in which words are spoken in a rhythm over a muscial background

rival (RYE-vuhl) · someone you compete against

sci-fi (SYE-FYE) · short for science fiction; a story about life in the future or on other planets

single (SING-guhl) · one song from an album; often played on the radio to get a new album noticed

soap opera (SOHP OP-er-uh) · a television series showing characters in overly dramatic ways

soulful (SOHL-fuhl) · filled with spirit or feelings of love

soundtrack (SOUND-trak) · the recorded music of a movie or play

tour (toor) · a trip made by musicians to perform in various places

Index